The Gut-Brain Link

Restoring Digestive Health for Mental Wellness

Harmony Royce

DEDICATION

This book is dedicated to everyone who wants to learn more about the complex relationship between the mind and body and who understands how important it is to take care of both in order to truly be well. To those who bravely set out on their own paths to self-discovery and healing, and to the gut-brain research pioneers whose curiosity and commitment keep unlocking new insights.

I hope that this work will be a resource for everyone who wants to embrace the gut-brain connection transforming power, bringing about long-lasting change, empowerment, and hope. I want to express my gratitude to my mentors, family, and friends for their constant belief in me and support.

And above all, to the reader: may your exploration of the deep and transforming relationship between the stomach and the brain bring you understanding, healing, and a refreshed sense of balance.

DISCLAIMER

This book's content is meant purely for educational reasons and isn't meant to identify, treat, or cure any illnesses. Although every attempt has been made to guarantee the authenticity of the information provided, the publisher and author disclaim all responsibility for any possible consequences that may result from using the advice or instructions provided.

It is highly advised that you speak with a skilled healthcare provider before making any changes to your food, lifestyle, or health routine, especially if you are pregnant or nursing, have pre-existing medical conditions, or are taking medication.

At the time of release, this book's content reflected the state of knowledge regarding the gut-brain connection. Since scientific research is always changing, the author advises readers to keep themselves updated and look for current information from reliable sources.

CONTENTS

ACKNOWLEDGMENTS..1

CHAPTER 1..1

The Gut-Brain Axis: An Overview...1

   1.1 The Gut-Brain Axis: What is It?.....................................1

   1.2 The Microbiome's Function...3

   1.3 Important Gut-Brain Communication Elements............5

CHAPTER 2..8

Gut Health and Mental Health Science................................8

   2.1 The Connection Between Mood Disorders and Gut Dysbiosis........8

   2.2 The Gut Produces Neurotransmitters.........................11

   2.3 New Research and Its Consequences...........................14

CHAPTER 3..18

Signs of a Troubled Gut-Brain Relationship.....................18

   3.1 Outward Symptoms of Digestive Disorders.................18

   3.2 Symptoms of Mental Health..21

   3.3 Indicators of Behavior..24

CHAPTER 4..28

Identifying Digestive Disorders..28

   4.1 Common Medical Examinations..................................28

   4.2 Assessing Effects on Mental Health.............................32

   4.3 Functional Medicine's Function...................................35

CHAPTER 5..40

Gut and Mental Health Nutrition..40

5.1 How Diet Affects the Microbiome...40

5.2 Foods to Steer Clear of to Promote Gut Healing........................... 44

5.3 Formulating a Diet Plan That Promotes Gut Health......................47

CHAPTER 6...**52**

Modifications to Lifestyle to Promote Gut-Brain Health......................**52**

6.1 Strategies for Stress Management...52

6.2 Physical Activity and Exercise... 56

6.3 Circadian Rhythm Alignment and Sleep....................................... 58

CHAPTER 7...**63**

Probiotics and Psychobiotics: Their Impact on Mental Health.............**63**

7.1 Psychobiotics: What Are They?...63

7.2 Food Sources versus Supplements..68

7.3 Psychobiotics' Clinical Support... 71

CHAPTER 8...**75**

Leaky Gut Syndrome Recovery...**75**

8.1 Leaky Gut Syndrome: What Is It?.. 75

8.2 Gut Lining Repair Procedures... 79

8.3 The Relationship Between Mood and Autoimmune Disorders...... 83

CHAPTER 9...**87**

Gut-Brain Connection Personalized Medicine.................................**87**

9.1 Adapting Interventions to Specific Requirements......................... 88

9.2 Mental Health Integrative Approaches... 91

9.3 Monitoring and Modifying for Extended Achievement.................. 94

CHAPTER 10..**98**

Gut-Brain Research and Applications in the Future...........................**98**

10.1 Developments in the Analysis of Microbiomes............98

10.2 Emerging Treatment Systems........................... 102

10.3 Useful Lessons for Daily Living...............................105

ABOUT THE AUTHOR...**109**

ACKNOWLEDGMENTS

My sincere appreciation goes out to everyone who helped and encouraged me while I was writing this book. First and foremost, to my friends and family, who have always been a source of strength with their unfailing love, tolerance, and support. This effort would not have been possible if you hadn't believed in me.

We are especially grateful to the professionals, scholars, and trailblazers in the domains of mental health, neuroscience, and gut health. The groundwork for this book was laid by your seminal research, which also offered priceless insight into the intricate and intriguing connection between the stomach and the brain. Thank you very much for sharing your wisdom with the world.

I want to express my gratitude to my peers, mentors, and coworkers for their support and for pushing me to reflect carefully and critically on the subjects covered. Your helpful criticism has been crucial in improving the content and making sure it satisfies the highest requirements for quality.

We appreciate the readers' interest, candor, and dedication to comprehending the complex relationships within their own bodies. I hope this book will be a helpful tool for you as you work to improve your health and wellbeing.

Finally, I want to express my gratitude to everyone who is putting forth endless effort to improve our awareness of the gut-brain relationship. Your contributions keep changing lives and inspiring others.

Many thanks to all of you.

CHAPTER 1

THE GUT-BRAIN AXIS: AN OVERVIEW

1.1 The Gut-Brain Axis: What is It?

The enteric nervous system (ENS), which regulates gastrointestinal processes, and the central nervous system (CNS), which is mostly the brain, are connected via the dynamic and complex gut-brain axis. The stomach and brain maintain a continuous dialogue thanks to this bidirectional communication, which also helps to coordinate a number of physiological and psychological processes.

The Gut-Brain Communication System in Both Directions

Complex immunological, hormonal, and neurological mechanisms mediate this communication. The stomach provides feedback to the brain that shapes mood, behavior, and cognitive processes, whereas the brain sends signals to the gut that affect motility, secretion, and absorption. According to new research, this connection is deeper than previously believed, and disorders including anxiety, sadness, and irritable bowel syndrome (IBS) are caused by abnormalities in gut-brain communication.

Function of the Enteric Nervous System and Vagus Nerve

A key component of the gut-brain axis is the vagus nerve, a cranial nerve that runs from the brainstem to the belly. The vagus nerve serves as a superhighway for communication, carrying sensory data from the gut to the brain and back again. For example:

- **Gut-to-Brain Signals:** The brain receives information from sensory receptors in the gut about changes in microbial activity, pH, and nutritional content.
- **Brain-to-Gut Signals:** The gut's response to stress and emotional states is influenced by the brain's vagal signals, which also affect digestive processes.

The ENS, sometimes referred to as the "second brain," is made up of more than 100 million neurons that are buried in the stomach lining and serve to supplement the vagus nerve. Numerous digestion processes are independently regulated by these neurons, which also interact with the central nervous system to affect mood and thought processes.

1.2 The Microbiome's Function

A key component of the gut-brain axis is the gut microbiome, a huge and varied ecology of bacteria that live in the gastrointestinal tract. These microbes, which include viruses, fungus, and bacteria, contribute to a delicate equilibrium that affects mental and physical health.

The Impact of Gut Bacteria on Mental Health

The synthesis of neurotransmitters and other substances that impact brain function is greatly aided by gut flora. For example:

- The production of serotonin, sometimes known as the "feel-good neurotransmitter," occurs in the stomach to the extent that it accounts for around 90% of the body's production. Serotonin production is associated with some bacteria, including

Lactobacillus and Bifidobacterium.

- **SCFAs (short-chain fatty acids):** SCFAs, such as butyrate and acetate, which are produced when microorganisms ferment dietary fiber, have anti-inflammatory qualities that affect how the brain works.

Research indicates that dysbiosis, or abnormalities in the gut microbiota, can result in inflammation, altered neurotransmitter levels, and increased gut permeability, or leaky gut, all of which are associated with mood disorders including anxiety and depression.

Variations in the Microbiome Composition of Anxious and Healthy People

In contrast to their healthy counterparts, people with mental health issues have different microbiome profiles, according to research:

- **Healthy Individuals:** Usually have robust and varied microbiomes that are full of good bacteria such as Bifidobacterium longum and Lactobacillus rhamnosus.
- **Depressed/Anxious People:** Frequently show lower

levels of anti-inflammatory species, more pathogenic bacteria, and less microbial diversity. The therapeutic potential of the microbiome in regulating mental health is demonstrated by the capacity of probiotics, prebiotics, and dietary treatments to restore equilibrium in the gut microbiota.

1.3 Important Gut-Brain Communication Elements

The brain and gut may communicate easily thanks to a number of biological systems, each of which has its own mechanisms that affect mental and physical well-being.

Gut-Produced Neurotransmitters

The synthesis of neurotransmitters, which control mood and cognitive processes, is greatly influenced by the gut flora.

- **Dopamine:** Dopamine is produced by some gut bacteria and affects motivation and reward processing.
- A neurotransmitter that encourages relaxation and lowers anxiety, gamma-aminobutyric acid (GABA) is produced by some strains, such as *Lactobacillus*

and Bifidobacterium.

- As was previously mentioned, gut-derived serotonin affects sleep, mood, and gastrointestinal motility.

To affect the brain, these neurotransmitters either activate neuronal pathways or reach the bloodstream.

The Impact of Hormonal Signals Like Cortisol

Cortisol, the body's main stress hormone, is a key player in the hormonal signaling that also affects the gut-brain axis.

- By increasing gut permeability and letting dangerous compounds enter the bloodstream, chronic stress can impair gut function.
- The mix of microorganisms is changing, favoring harmful germs.
- Inflammation results from a decrease in the formation of the protecting gut mucosa.

On the other hand, a balanced gut microbiota can control cortisol levels, preventing harm to the body and brain from stress.

A strong and intricate system that demonstrates the connection between mental and physical health is the gut-brain axis. Gaining insight into the functions of the gut microbiota, enteric nervous system, vagus nerve, and the complex communication routes they mediate opens up exciting possibilities for therapeutic intervention. The importance of preserving gut health as a foundation for general well-being is shown by the ongoing evolution of research in this area.

CHAPTER 2

GUT HEALTH AND MENTAL HEALTH SCIENCE

2.1 The Connection Between Mood Disorders and Gut Dysbiosis

A strong connection between gut health and mental health has been demonstrated by growing scientific data over the last ten years, with a special emphasis on the illness known as **gut dysbiosis**. This phrase describes an imbalance in the community of bacteria, fungi, viruses, and other microorganisms that live in the digestive system, known as the gut microbiota. The start and development of many mental health disorders, particularly anxiety and depression, are thought to be significantly influenced by dysbiosis.

Proof from Clinical Research on Depression and Anxiety

The composition of the gut microbiota and mental health

have been the subject of numerous clinical investigations, which have shown strong correlations. Researchers have discovered that when compared to healthy people, people with mood disorders including anxiety and depression frequently have different microbiome profiles.

- One of the most consistent findings is that people who suffer from anxiety and depression typically have gut microbiomes that are less diverse. Higher levels of pro-inflammatory markers and a decline in beneficial bacteria like Bifidobacterium and Lactobacillus species are frequently associated with a lack of variety.
- **Gut Microbial Transplants:** Research has also looked into fecal microbiota transplants (FMT), which include transferring a healthy person's gut microbiome to a depressed person. Numerous patients have reported notable improvements in their mood and emotional management, indicating that these investigations have produced favorable results. This supports the notion that mental health is directly impacted by the gut microbiome.

Because gut dysbiosis disrupts the gut-brain axis, a bidirectional communication network between the gut and the brain, researchers think it may have a role in the development of mood disorders. The beginning of mental health problems can be attributed to this disruption, which can also lead to inflammation, modifications in neurotransmitter synthesis, and changes in stress response systems.

Inflammation's Function

Inflammation is one of the primary ways that gut dysbiosis affects mental health. Immune cells that lining the stomach keep an eye on the body and defend it against dangerous infections. An inflammatory response can be triggered by dangerous bacteria when the gut microbiota becomes unbalanced. Pro-inflammatory cytokines and other immune molecules may rise as a result of this reaction, and they may enter the bloodstream and reach the brain, where they may contribute to neuroinflammation.

- **Systemic Inflammation:** Depression and other mood disorders have been associated with chronic inflammation. Depression and anxiety symptoms can result from inflammatory chemicals, including cytokines, interacting with the brain's neurotransmitter systems and passing through the blood-brain barrier.

- Gut dysbiosis frequently leads to increased intestinal permeability, which is also known as "leaky gut." Toxins and bacteria can enter the circulation through the gut barrier, causing inflammation and an immunological reaction that impairs brain function. Depression and other mood disorders are thought to emerge mostly as a result of this mechanism.

2.2 The Gut Produces Neurotransmitters

The stomach actively produces neurotransmitters that have a direct impact on the brain, making it more than just a passive organ involved in digesting. The stomach really produces a sizable amount of the body's neurotransmitters, underscoring the close connection between mental health and gut health.

90% of Serotonin's Production Takes Place in the Gut
serotonin, sometimes known as the "feel-good"

neurotransmitter because of its function in controlling mood, hunger, and sleep, is one of the most well-known neurotransmitters made in the gut. Surprisingly, the gut lining and enteric nervous system (ENS) of the gastrointestinal tract create almost 90% of the serotonin in the body.

- **Gut Microbial Influence:** The generation of serotonin is significantly influenced by the gut microbiota. Serotonin production is aided by some gut bacteria, including *Bifidobacterium* and *Lactobacillus*. These microorganisms affect the synthesis of tryptophan, a precursor amino acid to serotonin, and help convert it into serotonin. A steady and well-balanced mood is facilitated by appropriate serotonin levels, which are supported by a balanced gut microbiota.

- **Mood Control:** Anxiety, anger, and depression are linked to low serotonin levels in the brain. Thus, a dysbiosis of the gut microbiota might lower the production of serotonin, which can worsen mood disorders. New therapy strategies, such as using probiotics to enhance gut health and, consequently, mental health, have been spurred by the discovery of the connection between mood disorders and serotonin produced in the gut.

The Relaxing Effects of Gamma-Aminobutyric Acid (GABA)

Gamma-aminobutyric acid, or GABA, is another important neurotransmitter that is made in the stomach and is essential for reducing brain activity and encouraging relaxation. As the key inhibitory neurotransmitter in the brain, GABA is crucial for preserving composure and controlling anxiety because it lowers neuronal excitability.

- The Function of the Gut Microbiome in the Production of GABA Studies have demonstrated that some gut bacteria, including Lactobacillus rhamnosus, are capable of producing GABA. By encouraging the release of GABA, which lowers stress and anxiety, these good bacteria can directly affect brain activity. This demonstrates how emotional control can be directly impacted by the gut microbiota's ability to regulate the central nervous system.

- **Soothing Impacts**: Reductions in stress and anxiety symptoms are linked to higher GABA levels in the brain. It might be feasible to increase GABA production and encourage a more tranquil, balanced emotional state by cultivating a healthy gut microbiota.

2.3 New Research and Its Consequences

The future of mental health treatment is being shaped by several promising advances as the gut-brain connection continues to be studied. New therapeutic approaches, such as microbiome transplants and the developing discipline of psychobiotics, have been made possible by our increasing awareness of the gut microbiome's involvement in mental health.

Mood Enhancements and Microbiome Transplants

Fecal material from a healthy person is transferred into the gut of a person with mood disorders in a novel technique called a microbiome transplant, sometimes referred to as fecal microbiota transplantation (FMT). Restoring a healthy balance of gut flora is the aim in order to alleviate symptoms related to mental health. Numerous studies have demonstrated that FMT can help patients with anxiety, sadness, and other mental illnesses significantly improve their mood and emotional regulation.

- **Proof of Concept:** Studies have shown that FMT can reduce depressive symptoms and cause significant alterations in the composition of the gut flora. According to one study, patients who received microbiome transplants from healthy donors reported feeling happier and experiencing less symptoms of depression, indicating a link between mental and gut health.
- Despite its potential, FMT is still a topic of ongoing research, and standardizing the process and guaranteeing its safety present difficulties. Nonetheless, the increasing amount of data demonstrating FMT highlights the revolutionary potential of gut-based mental health treatments.

Innovative Research in Psychobiotics

The study of the therapeutic potential of probiotics beneficial microorganisms that have a favorable impact on mental health is the focus of the developing area of psychobiotics. Psychobiotics work by using probiotics to change the gut microbiota, which affects how the brain works and elevates mood.

- **Probiotics and Mood Regulation** Research has shown that some probiotic strains, such Lactobacillus and Bifidobacterium, can affect the generation of neurotransmitters, lower inflammation, and improve the gut-brain communication network, all of which can help control mood. These probiotics can be taken as supplements or as fermented foods such as kimchi, kefir, and yogurt.

- **Potential for Treating Anxiety and Depression**: Preliminary research on psychobiotics has demonstrated encouraging outcomes in lowering anxiety and depressive symptoms. These interventions, which focus on the gut microbiome, present a fresh, non-pharmacological method of treating mental health issues that may even be able to take the place of or supplement more conventional therapies like antidepressants.

Although research on the relationship between gut health and mental health is still in its early stages, it is obvious that our emotional and cognitive well-being are greatly influenced by our gut microbiota. The gut-brain axis is a potent force that affects mental health in ways we are only now learning about, from the synthesis of important neurotransmitters like serotonin and GABA to the significant consequences of gut dysbiosis on mood disorders. People who suffer from anxiety, depression, and other mood disorders may find new, efficient treatments thanks to emerging medicines like microbiota transplants and psychobiotics. Gut-based therapies will probably become a mainstay of mental health treatment in the future as our knowledge of this connection grows.

CHAPTER 3

Signs of a Troubled Gut-Brain Relationship

A complicated and intricate system, the gut-brain link has a big impact on mental and physical health. People may suffer from a variety of symptoms that impact not just the digestive system but also the mind and behavior when this relationship is disrupted. In order to clarify the ways in which gut health affects general wellbeing, this chapter examines the behavioral, mental, and physical symptoms that may result from a disruption in the gut-brain connection.

3.1 Outward Symptoms of Digestive Disorders

The most obvious signs of a disrupted gut-brain connection are frequently the physical ones, which can range from little discomfort to serious long-term illnesses. Trillions of microorganisms live in the gut, and when these bacteria, viruses, and fungi are out of balance, it can cause a number of systemic and digestive problems.

Constipation, diarrhea, and bloating

The most prevalent physical symptoms of digestive issues are bloating, diarrhea, and constipation among other digestive disorders. These symptoms frequently occur when the gut microbiome is out of balance, either due to a deficiency of beneficial microorganisms or an overabundance of dangerous bacteria.

- Bloating is the result of too much gas building up in the intestines and stomach. The fermentation of undigested food is the most prevalent cause, and it is more likely to occur when the gut microbiota is disturbed. Bloating, discomfort, and a feeling of fullness can result from digestive issues caused by an imbalance in gut flora.

- **Diarrhea:** Chronic diarrhea, in which the body excretes waste more frequently and in liquid form, can be caused by a disruption in the gut flora. This is frequently caused by an imbalance in gut flora, which can impair the intestines' capacity to adequately absorb nutrients and water.

On the other hand, constipation is another sign of a digestive disorder. The gastrointestinal tract may not work well when gut bacteria are out of balance, which can slow down bowel motions and make it harder to pass stools.

These symptoms are frequently associated with illnesses that can be impacted by the gut-brain axis, including leaky gut syndrome, inflammatory bowel disease (IBD), and irritable bowel syndrome (IBS). Maintaining proper digestive function depends on the gut's capacity to interact with the brain. It can cause a chain reaction of bodily pain and misery when disturbed.

Prolonged Fatigue and Inflammation

Many gut problems are characterized by chronic inflammation, which is a strong sign that the gut-brain link is disrupted. A significant amount of the body's immune system is located in the gut, and when it becomes inflamed, the immune system may be improperly activated, resulting in systemic inflammation.

- **Chronic Inflammation:** When the intestinal lining is destroyed, toxic substances can seep into the bloodstream, resulting in illnesses like leaky gut syndrome. In addition to the gut, other organs and systems, including the brain, may be impacted by the immunological response that this sets off.

- **Fatigue:** Systemic inflammation frequently coexists with chronic fatigue. Immune cells release proteins called inflammatory cytokines, which can directly affect the brain and change how people sleep and think. As a result, persons with gut-related inflammation commonly report persistent weariness, low energy levels, and difficulties sustaining focus.

Beyond the digestive tract, the body's inflammatory reaction to gut problems can impact other organ systems and cause symptoms including headaches, body aches, and exhaustion. This ongoing state of inflammation can exacerbate the vicious cycle of gut-brain dysfunction by making people feel exhausted, mentally disoriented, and physically lethargic.

3.2 Symptoms of Mental Health

In addition to causing physical discomfort, the gut-brain

link has a big impact on mental health. The vagus nerve, neurotransmitters, and immunological signals are all part of the intricate system that connects the gut microbiota to the brain. From mood issues to cognitive challenges, a disruption in the gut-brain axis can cause a variety of mental health symptoms.

Brain fog, depression, and anxiety

Anxiety, melancholy, and brain fog are the most prevalent mental health symptoms linked to a disrupted gut-brain connection. Gut dysbiosis, or an imbalance in the gut microbiome, frequently makes these illnesses worse.

- **Anxiety:** Studies have indicated that an overactive stress response, which can be a symptom of an imbalanced gut flora, can cause anxiety. The gut produces a considerable quantity of serotonin, the neurotransmitter involved in mood regulation, and when its production is interrupted, individuals may experience heightened emotions of anxiety.

- **Depression:** Depression is also closely associated with a disrupted gut-brain connection. A significant amount of the body's serotonin is produced in the gut, and disorders in the gut can cause the brain's serotonin levels to drop, which can exacerbate depressed symptoms.

- The term "brain fog" describes a group of cognitive symptoms, such as mental exhaustion, trouble focusing, and poor remembering. People with long-term digestive problems frequently exhibit this, as inflammation and interruption of neurotransmitter production affect cognitive function. Brain fog can make it tough to complete ordinary tasks and can be a substantial hindrance to mental clarity and concentration.

These mental health issues are based in the disruptions taking place in the gut and are not only psychological in nature. People may experience mental and emotional illness as a direct result of inflammation, gut dysbiosis, and altered neurotransmitter synthesis.

Association with Cognitive A decline

A disrupted gut-brain connection has also been connected to cognitive decline in addition to mood disorders. There is growing evidence that persistent gut inflammation and dysbiosis may contribute to neurodegenerative disorders such as Alzheimer's disease and Parkinson's disease.

- **Inflammation and Neurodegeneration:** Prolonged inflammation brought on by an unbalanced gut microbiota can affect the brain for a long time, causing damage to neurons and the buildup of plaques that are frequently observed in diseases like Alzheimer's. Gut-released inflammatory cytokines have the ability to enter the brain and cause neuroinflammation, which hastens the deterioration of brain tissue.

- **Cognitive Function and the Gut-Brain Axis**: Maintaining cognitive function, particularly memory and learning, depends on the brain-gut connection. A disruption in this relationship can affect cognitive function, resulting in a reduction in mental acuity and a higher chance of neurodegenerative disorders in later life.

3.3 Indicators of Behavior

In addition to physical and mental health concerns, persons

with a disrupted gut-brain connection often experience behavioral changes. These changes can include food cravings, emotional eating, and sleep difficulties, all of which have a major impact on daily living.

Emotional Eating and Food Cravings

There are multiple ways in which gut dysbiosis might impact emotional eating and food cravings. An imbalance in the gut microbiota might result in cravings for unhealthy or high-sugar foods because it plays a crucial role in controlling hunger and satiety signals.

- **Cravings for Sugar and Processed Foods:** People may develop cravings for sugar and processed foods due to the growth of certain harmful gut bacteria, which can affect the brain's reward system. This yearning loop has the potential to worsen digestive and mental health issues by upsetting the gut microbiota and promoting unhealthy eating patterns.

- **Emotional Eating:** Emotional eating is frequently a coping strategy used to manage depression, anxiety, or stress. Emotional control is closely linked to the gut-brain connection, and when the stomach is out of balance, people may use food as a coping mechanism. This loop can exacerbate mental and physical health problems by causing weight gain and bad eating habits.

Sleep Disorders and Their Effects on Cycles

The gut-brain axis also has a significant impact on sleep. Inadequate sleep can exacerbate gut health, and poor gut health can interfere with sleep cycles. This results in a vicious cycle that affects mental and physical health.

- **Gut Dysbiosis and Sleep Issues:** Studies have indicated that the production of neurotransmitters such as melatonin and serotonin, which are essential for controlling sleep, can be impacted by gut dysbiosis. An irregular sleep-wake cycle, insomnia, and poor sleep quality can all result from imbalances in the gut microbiota.
- **The Sleep-Gut Connection:** It is also commonly known that sleep disorders have an effect on gut health. The gut-brain link can be further disrupted by inadequate sleep, which can further increase intestinal permeability, cause inflammation, and alter

gut motility. Both physical and mental health issues can be exacerbated by this cycle of sleep disturbance and intestinal malfunction.

There are numerous physical, emotional, and behavioral symptoms that can indicate a disruption in the gut-brain connection. The influence of gut health on general well-being is significant, ranging from digestive problems like bloating and constipation to mental health issues like anxiety and brain fog. In order to treat these symptoms, one must comprehend the complex interrelationship between the gut microbiota and the brain and take action to reestablish equilibrium by dietary modifications, lifestyle adjustments, and focused therapies. People can actively work to improve their gut and mental health by identifying the symptoms of a disrupted gut-brain connection.

CHAPTER 4

IDENTIFYING DIGESTIVE DISORDERS

Our general health is greatly influenced by the gut-brain connection, and disruptions in this complex communication system can cause a variety of psychological and physical problems. A multimodal approach is necessary to diagnose gut-related problems, including conventional medical testing, evaluations of the effects on mental health, and holistic approaches that look at the underlying reasons. The diagnostic techniques for gut-related illnesses, their effects on mental health, and the role functional medicine plays in advancing a more thorough understanding of gut health are all covered in this chapter.

4.1 Common Medical Examinations

Standard medical tests that aid doctors in understanding the condition of the gastrointestinal tract are frequently the first step in diagnosing gut-related issues. These examinations can shed light on the gut's physical state and reveal any abnormalities or dysfunctions that may be impairing its functionality.

Microbiome Profiling and Stool Analysis

- **Stool analysis** is one of the main diagnostic methods used to evaluate gut health. This test looks at a stool sample's contents to find any anomalies that might point to a digestive issue. Several significant indicators of gastrointestinal function can be found by stool analysis:

- A stool test can reveal information about the kind and quantity of bacteria, fungi, viruses, and other microorganisms that make up the gut microbiota. According to research, inflammatory bowel disease (IBD), mood disorders, and irritable bowel syndrome (IBS) are frequently associated with **dysbiosis**, an imbalance in the microbiome. Healthcare professionals can better understand the microbial habitat in the gut and its possible effects on mental and physical health by examining the composition of the microbiome.

- The presence of dangerous organisms, such as viruses, parasites, or pathogenic bacteria (such Salmonella or Clostridium difficile), can also be detected by stool testing. These microorganisms have the ability to interfere with gut function, resulting in symptoms like bloating, diarrhea, and discomfort in the abdomen. Early detection of these pathogens can direct the best course of therapy and help avoid more difficulties.

- **Digestive Enzymes and Fat Malabsorption:** Deficits in digestive enzymes and indications of fat malabsorption, both of which point to weakened gut health, can also be found through stool examination. Weight loss, nutritional deficits, and gastrointestinal pain can result from malabsorption diseases.

Apart from stool examination, microbiome profiling has become a sophisticated method for comprehending the ecology of the gut. DNA sequencing methods are used in microbiome profiling to pinpoint the precise bacterial species that are found in the stomach. This approach offers more nuanced insights into how gut health may be affecting an individual's physical and mental well-being by providing comprehensive information about the ratio of good to bad bacteria.

Inflammation Marker Blood Tests

The existence of inflammation, a major contributing factor to many gut-related illnesses, can be evaluated with blood testing. Crohn's disease, ulcerative colitis, and IBS can all be exacerbated by chronic inflammation, which is frequently caused by gut dysbiosis. Blood testing can identify indicators such as the following that point to systemic inflammation:

- **C-Reactive Protein (CRP):** CRP is a typical indicator of inflammation that is raised in inflammatory disorders. Particularly in diseases like IBD, elevated CRP levels can indicate the existence of intestinal inflammation.

- An indicator of inflammation, the Erythrocyte Sedimentation Rate (ESR) test gauges how quickly red blood cells sink in a test tube. In inflammatory diseases, especially those that affect the stomach, ESR is frequently raised.

- **Antibody Tests:** Certain blood tests identify antibodies that might be increased in gut-related autoimmune diseases. For instance, blood testing can identify antibodies to gliadin or transglutaminase, which are frequently present in celiac disease. These indicators can aid in the diagnosis of digestive system-related autoimmune diseases.

Healthcare professionals can start to construct a picture of the gut's health and pinpoint underlying problems that might be causing gastrointestinal distress by combining stool analysis and blood tests.

4.2 Assessing Effects on Mental Health

It is not just a physical problem when the gut-brain link is disrupted. It can have a serious impact on mental health, exacerbating diseases like anxiety, depression, and cognitive loss. Thus, identifying gut-related problems requires assessing the psychological impact of gut health.

Anxiety and Depression Screening Resources

To evaluate anxiety and depression, mental health practitioners frequently employ particular screening tools. These instruments are standardized questionnaires that aid in determining the intensity of psychological symptoms and offer information on whether gut symptoms and mental health problems are related.

- **GAD-7, or generalized anxiety disorder 7:** One popular instrument for determining the intensity of anxiety symptoms is the GAD-7. Clinicians can determine if stomach abnormalities may increase anxiety by asking people to rate the frequency of anxiety-related symptoms they have encountered over the last two weeks.

- The PHQ-9, or Patient Health Questionnaire, is: A screening tool for determining the intensity of depression symptoms is the PHQ-9. It asks questions regarding mood, hunger, sleep, and focus—all of which can be impacted by digestive problems. In addition to digestive symptoms, people may have substantial mood or cognitive changes, which could indicate that gut dysfunction is a contributing factor to their mental health issues.

- When individuals have both mental health symptoms and gastrointestinal problems at the same time, these screening methods can be especially beneficial. An in-depth assessment of the patient's mental health can assist in identifying the underlying causes of sadness and anxiety as well as any potential connections to gastrointestinal disorders.

Linking Psychological Disorders to Gut Symptoms

Knowing how gut symptoms connect to psychological disorders is a crucial first step in detecting gut-related mental health consequences. Studies have indicated that disorders such as anxiety and depression are not just caused by psychological variables, but are also significantly impacted by gut health.

- The production of neurotransmitters like serotonin, which are essential for mood regulation, might be impacted by an imbalance in gut flora, as was previously discussed. Depression is frequently linked to low serotonin levels, and gut dysbiosis might decrease this crucial neurotransmitter's availability. In a similar vein, long-term intestinal inflammation can interfere with the brain's emotional regulation, increasing stress and anxiety reactions.

- Cognitive Function The gut also affects the brain's cognitive processes, including memory, concentration, and judgment. Brain fog, memory loss, and concentration problems are typical in people with chronic gut illnesses like IBS or IBD, and they can be exacerbated by a disruption in the gut-brain link.

Clinicians can treat patients more holistically by addressing both the physical and psychological facets of their health by linking mental health symptoms to digestive problems.

4.3 Functional Medicine's Function

Conventional medical diagnostics concentrate on treating

particular diseases or disorders and their symptoms. On the other hand, functional medicine adopts a more comprehensive strategy, seeking to find the underlying causes of health problems as opposed to only treating their symptoms. When it comes to gut-related conditions, functional medicine is crucial in identifying underlying abnormalities that traditional testing can miss.

Comprehensive Methods for Diagnosis

Practitioners of functional medicine examine the body holistically, taking into account the relationships between the immunological, neurological, endocrine, and digestive systems. Functional medicine uses the following methods to diagnose gut-related conditions:

- **Factors related to diet and lifestyle:** A key element of functional medicine is a comprehensive assessment of a patient's environmental, dietary, and lifestyle choices. Stress, physical activity, sleep patterns, and diet (processed foods, sugar, and gluten) are all associated with a number of digestive problems. Restoring the gut-brain connection may include recognizing and changing these variables.

- **Allergies and Food Sensitivities:** Tests that gauge the body's immunological reaction to particular foods are frequently used in functional medicine to diagnose food sensitivities or allergies. These sensitivities have the potential to disturb the gut microbiota and cause inflammation. Both physical and mental health can significantly improve with the identification and removal of trigger foods.

- Long-term exposure to environmental pollutants, including chemicals, herbicides, and heavy metals, can damage gut health. Practitioners of functional medicine may employ tests to determine the body's toxin levels and suggest detoxification techniques to aid in gut healing.

Finding the Root Causes Outside of Traditional Tests

Functional medicine seeks to identify underlying imbalances that might be causing gut-related problems in addition to addressing dietary and lifestyle factors. These consist of:

- **Leaky Gut Syndrome (Gut Permeability):** This condition is characterized by damage to the intestinal lining, which permits toxic substances to seep into the circulation. In order to restore gut integrity, practitioners of functional medicine may employ specialized tests to detect gut permeability and suggest remedies like probiotics, healing herbs, or particular dietary adjustments.

- **Hormonal Imbalances:** Thyroid, sex, and cortisol hormones are among the hormones that can affect gut health. Given the importance of hormonal balance in gut health, functional medicine may employ tests to assess hormone levels and correct any imbalances that may be impacting the gut and the brain.

Functional medicine offers a more thorough and customized method of identifying and treating gut-related illnesses by concentrating on these underlying causes, assisting patients in achieving long-lasting health gains.

A comprehensive, multifaceted approach that incorporates

functional medicine, mental health assessments, and regular medical testing is necessary to diagnose gut-related problems. Blood testing and stool analysis can reveal information on the physical condition of the gut, and mental health evaluations can reveal the psychological effects of intestinal dysfunction. In order to identify underlying imbalances and advance general well-being, functional medicine is crucial. Healthcare professionals can gain a deeper understanding of the intricate relationships between the stomach and brain by employing these diverse diagnostic techniques, which will ultimately result in more efficient therapies and enhanced patient health results.

CHAPTER 5

GUT AND MENTAL HEALTH NUTRITION

Scientific study is becoming more interested in the connection between gut health, diet, and mental health. Through the gut-brain axis, it is widely known that the gut microbiota has a significant impact on mental health in addition to digestive health. This chapter examines how nutrition affects the microbiome, lists foods that can help or hurt gut health, and provides helpful advice for developing a gut-healthy diet that supports mental and physical wellness.

5.1 How Diet Affects the Microbiome

Numerous facets of health are significantly impacted by the human microbiome, which is the collection of billions of microorganisms that reside in the gut. Recent studies have shed light on how our diets can directly impact the equilibrium of these microbial communities, which in turn can impact immunological responses, gut function, and even brain health.

Foods High in Fiber to Maintain a Healthy Gut Lining

The foundation of a healthy gut microbiome is dietary fiber. As a prebiotic, fiber feeds the good bacteria in the gut, promoting their growth and preserving their equilibrium. Gut bacteria digest most fiber in the colon, generating short-chain fatty acids (SCFAs) such acetate, propionate, and butyrate. Because they sustain the mucosal barrier, which keeps dangerous substances out of the bloodstream, SCFAs are essential for preserving the integrity of the gut lining.

- One SCFA that is especially crucial for gut health is butyrate. It helps heal the intestinal lining, lowers inflammation, and feeds colon cells. Conditions like leaky gut syndrome, in which chemicals and pathogens enter the circulation through holes in the intestinal wall and cause systemic inflammation and a host of health issues, including anxiety and depression can be avoided with a healthy gut lining.

- **Sources of Fiber** Whole grains, legumes, fruits, and vegetables are foods high in fiber. Foods high in soluble and insoluble fiber include, for instance, apples, bananas, broccoli, beans, oats, and quinoa. A balanced and healthy gut microbiome is supported by including these foods high in fiber in the diet.

- In addition to enhancing gut health, a high-fiber diet also promotes the creation of mood-regulating neurotransmitters like serotonin, lowers inflammation, and controls blood sugar levels, all of which enhance mental wellness.

Probiotic Benefits of Fermented Foods

Probiotics, which are live bacteria that can provide health advantages when ingested in sufficient quantities, are abundant in fermented meals. Probiotics are essential for maintaining the microbiome's equilibrium, enhancing digestion, and encouraging the synthesis of SCFAs, which support the gut lining.

- It has been demonstrated that some strains of lactic acid bacteria (LAB), which are present in fermented foods, enhance gut health and lessen the symptoms of gastrointestinal illnesses. Through the gut-brain axis, these helpful bacteria can also communicate with the brain, potentially reducing depressive and anxious feelings.

- **Sources of Fermented Foods:** Yogurt, kefir, kimchi, sauerkraut, miso, and kombucha are examples of common fermented foods. In addition to improving the gut microbiota, these meals offer extra nutrients, such as B vitamins, that promote mental health and mental wellness. A resilient microbiome depends on the diversity of gut bacteria, which can be increased by consuming a range of fermented foods.

By regulating gut bacteria, lowering inflammation, and improving nutrient absorption, fermented foods can help benefit mental health. They are an essential component of a gut-healthy diet. This could therefore have a favorable effect on mood, thinking, and general mental health.

5.2 Foods to Steer Clear of to Promote Gut Healing

Certain foods promote gut health, but others can upset the delicate balance of the gut flora and lead to mental health issues, inflammation, and gut permeability. Maintaining a healthy gut-brain relationship requires knowing which foods to avoid.

Artificial Sweeteners and Processed Foods

Highly processed meals are frequently loaded with harmful fats, artificial sweeteners, added sugars, and preservatives, all of which can have a detrimental effect on gut health and the microbiota.

- A diet heavy in added sugars may encourage the growth of pathogenic bacteria and fungi, causing dysbiosis, or an imbalance in the microbiome. Consuming a lot of sugar has also been connected to increased inflammation and gut permeability, which can exacerbate illnesses like leaky gut and systemic inflammation. Anxiety and depression are two mental health conditions that are frequently linked to this persistent low-grade inflammation.

- **Artificial Sweeteners:** Aspartame, saccharin, and sucralose are examples of artificial sweeteners that are frequently present in processed meals and diet items. According to studies, these sweeteners can change the gut microbiome by encouraging the growth of bad bacteria and reducing the number of good bacteria. Mood swings, digestive problems, and metabolic disorders can all be made more likely by this imbalance.

- **Unhealthy Fats:** Omega-6 fatty acids and trans fats, which are present in a lot of processed snacks, fast food, and baked products, can cause inflammation in the body and the gut. Both gastrointestinal disorders and mental health issues, such as depression, are significantly increased by chronic inflammation.

Reducing inflammation and preserving a balanced gut microbiome require avoiding processed meals and artificial sugars. Gut and mental health will be supported by a diet high in whole, unprocessed foods.

The Controversial Function of Gluten in Gut Permeability

There is continuous discussion on gluten's impact on gut health. Although it is commonly known that people with celiac disease or non-celiac gluten sensitivity needs to stay away from gluten, research is currently ongoing to determine how gluten may affect the guts of those without these disorders.

- **Gluten Sensitivity and Leaky Gut:** According to some study, those who are sensitive to gluten may experience leaky gut, or increased intestinal permeability. Toxins and inflammatory chemicals seep into the bloodstream as a result of the gut lining's impaired integrity in leaky gut syndrome. Widespread inflammation may result from this, impacting mental and physical well-being.

- **Possible Consequences for Mental Health:** There is mounting evidence that mental health conditions like anxiety, sadness, and cognitive dysfunction are associated with gluten sensitivity. For some who are sensitive to gluten, removing it from their diet may alleviate symptoms, while further research is required to completely understand the reasons.

Reducing or eliminating gluten may be helpful for people who are having mental health or digestive problems, especially if gluten sensitivity or leaky gut is suspected. However, before making big nutritional changes, it's crucial to speak with a healthcare provider.

5.3 Formulating a Diet Plan That Promotes Gut Health

A balanced, anti-inflammatory, and nutrient-dense eating pattern that promotes gut and mental health is part of a gut-healthy diet plan, in addition to incorporating foods that support the microbiota. Choosing anti-inflammatory foods, keeping a varied and varied diet, and balancing macronutrients are all doable stages in developing such a plan.

Doable Actions to Maintain Macronutrient Balance

Overall health, including gut health, depends on a balanced diet that contains the right proportions of macronutrients fats, proteins, and carbs.

- **Carbohydrates**: Avoid processed carbohydrates and refined sugars in favor of complex carbohydrates found in whole grains, fruits, and vegetables. As was previously mentioned, the fiber in these foods nourishes good gut flora and encourages the synthesis of SCFAs.

- Lean meats, fish, eggs, legumes, and plant-based proteins like quinoa and tofu are all excellent sources of protein that help the body's immune system and heal damaged tissue. Additionally, protein is required for the synthesis of neurotransmitters and enzymes that promote brain and intestinal health.

- **Fats:** Good fats, especially omega-3 fatty acids, which are present in walnuts, flaxseeds, and fatty fish (such salmon and mackerel), aid promote brain function and lower inflammation. In the brain and intestines, these lipids are essential for preserving the integrity of cell membranes.

- Promoting intestinal health and mental well-being requires striking a balance between these macronutrients while emphasizing entire, nutrient-dense diets.

Including Components That Reduce Inflammation

A common characteristic of many mental and gut-related illnesses is chronic inflammation. Including anti-inflammatory foods in the diet can promote gut and brain health and assist lower systemic inflammation.

- **Turmeric:** The active ingredient in turmeric, curcumin, has potent antioxidant and anti-inflammatory qualities. It has been demonstrated to lessen intestinal inflammation and may help alleviate the symptoms of inflammatory bowel disease (IBD) and IBS. Curcumin has also been connected to improvements in mood disorders like anxiety and sadness.

- Similar to turmeric, ginger has been demonstrated to have anti-inflammatory properties that promote intestinal health. It can lessen nausea, ease stomach discomfort, and enhance intestinal motility in general.

- **Leafy Greens and Berries:** Antioxidants and anti-inflammatory chemicals are abundant in dark leafy greens, such as Swiss chard, spinach, and kale. Antioxidants included in berries, such as strawberries and blueberries, help shield the brain and intestines from inflammation and oxidative damage.

People can boost mental health and intestinal health by including these anti-inflammatory foods in their diet.

Gut and mental health are fundamentally influenced by nutrition. In addition to protecting the gut lining and lowering systemic inflammation, a diet high in fiber, fermented foods, and anti-inflammatory substances can also support a healthy microbiome. However, limiting processed foods, artificial sweeteners, and gluten (if you're susceptible) will help avoid inflammation and gut dysbiosis, which can lead to mental health problems. People can enhance their digestive system and general mental health by developing a nutrient-dense, well-balanced diet that supports gut health. In the end, a gut-healthy diet is an effective way to promote mental and physical well-being.

CHAPTER 6

MODIFICATIONS TO LIFESTYLE TO PROMOTE GUT-BRAIN HEALTH

An increasing amount of research emphasizes the vital link between the gut and the brain, showing how lifestyle choices like stress reduction, exercise, and sleep may have a big impact on both mental and digestive health. This chapter explores lifestyle modifications that can support gut-brain health, emphasizing the value of restorative sleep, stress reduction strategies, and the advantages of exercise. People can enhance mental health, lower gut inflammation, and maintain a healthy microbiome by comprehending and putting these tactics into practice.

6.1 Strategies for Stress Management

Both gut health and mental health are significantly impacted by stress, especially chronic stress. The gut-brain axis is a bidirectional communication system that connects the brain's central nervous system to the gut's enteric nervous system, forming an intricate connection between the two organs. Chronic stress can interfere with this connection, resulting in a number of digestive problems, including bloating, IBS, and even gastrointestinal illnesses like ulcers. Furthermore, mental health issues like depression and anxiety can be made worse by stress.

Chronic Stress's Effect on Gut Function

Prolonged stress causes the body to release stress chemicals like cortisol and adrenaline, which trigger the fight-or-flight response. The balance of gut bacteria can be upset, intestinal permeability can be increased (resulting in leaky gut), and gut motility can be changed by these hormones. In addition to decreasing mucus production in the gut lining, elevated cortisol levels can also decrease the barrier that prevents dangerous substances from entering the bloodstream. Systemic inflammation may result from this, causing mental health issues as well as gastrointestinal complaints.

- Stress can cause either an increase in gastrointestinal motility, which can result in diarrhea, or a decrease in it, which can result in constipation. The digestive tract is disturbed by this erratic motility, which results in pain and inadequate absorption of nutrients.

- **Imbalance of the Gut Microbiome:** It has been demonstrated that long-term stress changes the makeup and diversity of the gut microbiome, decreasing the number of good bacteria and increasing the number of dangerous ones. This dysbiosis can have a detrimental impact on mental health and exacerbate gastrointestinal problems.

Yoga and Mindfulness and How They Affect the Vagus Nerve

Yoga and mindfulness are useful techniques for promoting gut-brain health and stress management. These activities mitigate the effects of chronic stress by activating the parasympathetic nervous system, also referred to as the rest-and-digest system. By fostering present-moment awareness, mindfulness lessens the harmful effects of thinking and promotes calm. Yoga improves the body's capacity to manage stress, particularly when it is combined with deep breathing, positions, and relaxation techniques.

- **Vagus Nerve Activation:** A vital part of the parasympathetic nervous system, the vagus nerve is activated by both yoga and mindfulness. By encouraging gut motility and preserving the integrity of the gut lining, the vagus nerve plays a critical role in controlling gut function. Additionally, it affects the synthesis of neurotransmitters like serotonin, which are essential for controlling mood.

- **Mindfulness Practices:** It has been demonstrated that mindfulness practices, such guided meditation and focused breathing, lower stress hormones and enhance gut health. These techniques support the restoration of a balanced gut flora and help control the body's stress response.

- People can improve intestinal health, increase mental well-being, and become more resilient to stress by implementing yoga and mindfulness into their daily lives.

6.2 Physical Activity and Exercise

Another important factor in gut-brain health is regular exercise. Exercise has a profound impact on mental and digestive health. In addition to improving physical health, studies have revealed that movement affects the gut microbiota's composition and the synthesis of neurotransmitters that control mood and thought processes.

The Benefits of Movement for Gut Motility

Healthy digestion depends on intestinal motility, which is stimulated by exercise. Engaging in physical exercise speeds up the passage of food and waste through the digestive tract and improves blood flow to the intestines. This encourages regular waste removal, lowers the chance of constipation, and supports a healthy gut flora.

- **Improved Digestion:** By increasing the rate at which food passes through the intestines, regular exercise can help maintain good digestive function and avoid problems like indigestion and bloating.

- **Decreased Inflammation:** Exercise also contains

anti-inflammatory properties, which can be especially helpful for people with inflammatory bowel disease (IBD), leaky gut, or IBS. Exercise promotes mental and gastrointestinal health by lowering systemic inflammation.

- The release of endorphins, the body's natural mood-enhancing chemicals, is a major factor in the broad recognition of exercise's positive effects on mental health. Endorphins are neurotransmitters that contribute to emotions of euphoria and less pain perception. Better mood, less anxiety, and an overall increase in mental health can result from this.

- **Stress Reduction:** Exercise counteracts the harmful effects of stress by releasing endorphins. Frequent exercise can improve the balance of gut flora and lessen the effects of everyday stressors, resulting in a lasting sense of wellbeing.

- It has been demonstrated that exercise encourages neurogenesis, or the development of new neurons in the brain. This can help prevent mood disorders including depression and cognitive decline while also enhancing cognitive performance.

- Regular physical activity, such as swimming, running, walking, or strength training, improves digestion, lowers inflammation, and increases mood-enhancing endorphins, all of which support gut and mental health.

6.3 Circadian Rhythm Alignment and Sleep

Sleep is necessary for the body, particularly the gut, to heal and regenerate. The gut lining is one of the cells in the body that is repaired during restorative sleep. Additionally, because some microbial communities are more active when you sleep, sleep is essential for preserving the balance of the gut microbiome.

Restorative Sleep Is Essential for Gut Repair

Gut function is significantly impacted by the circadian rhythm of the body, which is controlled by the natural light-dark cycle. Impaired gut barrier function, abnormal gut motility, and an imbalance in gut flora can result from circadian rhythm disruptions, such as irregular sleep patterns or inadequate sleep. This can then lead to mental health problems and worsen the symptoms of digestive diseases.

- **Gut Lining Repair:** The body concentrates on cell regeneration and tissue repair as you sleep deeply. This involves repairing the intestinal lining, which is necessary to support the body's immune system and avoid leaky gut syndrome. Additionally, getting enough sleep promotes the synthesis of growth factors that support the integrity of the intestinal lining.

- **Microbiome Balance:** Sleep disturbances have been linked to alterations in the gut microbiome's makeup, namely a decrease in the variety of good bacteria. For healthy digestion, immunological response, and mental well-being, a varied and balanced microbiome is essential.

Advice for Better Sleep Practices

Prioritizing restful sleep is crucial for promoting both

mental and gastrointestinal health. The following advice can help you synchronize your circadian cycle and enhance your sleep hygiene:

- The body's circadian rhythm can be regulated by adhering to a regular sleep schedule, which involves going to bed and waking up at the same time each day. The secret to preserving sound sleep habits is consistency.

- Establish a Calm Sleeping Environment: Keep the room calm, dark, and cool to create a restful sleeping environment. Reducing exposure to blue light, which disrupts the synthesis of the sleep hormone melatonin, can be achieved by avoiding electronics like computers and smartphones right before bed.

- **Reduce Alcohol and Caffeine Consumption:** Alcohol and caffeine interfere with the body's capacity to go into deep sleep stages, which can cause sleep disturbances. Reducing these drugs can help you sleep better, especially in the evening.

- The body can be told when it's time to wind down and get ready for sleep by engaging in relaxing pre-sleep routines, such as reading, deep breathing, meditation, or listening to soothing music.

Those who prioritize restorative sleep and stick to a regular sleep pattern can improve mental health, balance the microbiota, and aid in gut repair.

In order to support digestive and mental health, lifestyle choices like stress reduction, exercise, and sleep are essential. Practices like yoga, vagus nerve stimulation, and mindfulness can help lessen the negative consequences of chronic stress, which can change the gut microbiota and impair gut function. While restorative sleep is necessary for gut repair and the maintenance of a healthy microbiome, regular physical activity increases gut motility, lowers inflammation, and increases mood-enhancing endorphins. People can maximize their gut-brain health and enhance their general well-being by consciously altering their lifestyles to prioritize stress reduction, exercise, and good sleep hygiene. These adjustments promote mental well-being and improve digestive function, resulting in a harmonious body-mind balance.

CHAPTER 7

PROBIOTICS AND PSYCHOBIOTICS: THEIR IMPACT ON MENTAL HEALTH

For a long time, the mind and gut were considered distinct entities, and mental health and bodily functions were frequently addressed separately. However, new research has revealed a critical link between mental health and gut health, leading to the development of a new specialty called psychobiotics. The function of psychobiotics probiotics that directly affect mental health is examined in this chapter, along with their processes, the distinction between diet and supplements, and the clinical data demonstrating their efficacy in treating mood disorders such as depression and anxiety.

7.1 Psychobiotics: What Are They?

Psychobiotics are a subclass of probiotics, which are live microorganisms that benefit the host and are specifically associated with better mental health. The foundation of this idea is the idea that the gut microbiota regulates brain function through the **gut-brain axis**, a sophisticated communication mechanism that links the gut and the brain. Because it produces neurotransmitters like dopamine and serotonin, which are crucial for mood regulation, the gut is frequently referred to as the "second brain."

Definition and Action Mechanisms

Psychobiotics have a beneficial impact on mental health by altering the gut-brain axis. When taken in sufficient amounts, these probiotics work with the gut flora to create metabolites and neurotransmitters that affect behavior and brain function. Several main pathways can be used to classify their mechanisms of action:

- The synthesis of important neurotransmitters, including serotonin, dopamine, and gamma-aminobutyric acid (GABA), can be influenced by a variety of probiotic strains. Often referred to as the "feel-good" neurotransmitter, serotonin is important for controlling mood, anxiety, and happiness. It's interesting to note that the stomach produces 90% of serotonin, indicating that a healthy microbiome is essential for its synthesis.

- **Inflammation Reduction:** Low-grade chronic inflammation has been linked to a number of mental health issues, such as depression and anxiety. By lowering gut-related inflammation and regulating the immune system, psychobiotics can lessen systemic inflammation that is connected to mental health issues.

- The Hypothalamic-Pituitary-Adrenal (HPA) Axis is regulated as follows: The body's reaction to stress is controlled by the HPA axis. Numerous mood disorders have been linked to this system's dysregulation. By modifying the HPA axis, psychobiotics might lessen the body's stress response and cortisol levels, which are known as the "stress hormone."

- **Gut Barrier Integrity:** To keep dangerous bacteria and inflammatory chemicals out of the bloodstream, a healthy gut barrier is necessary. By strengthening the mucosal lining and encouraging the growth of good bacteria, probiotics help preserve the integrity of the gut and lessen the risk of **leaky gut**. Psychobiotics have the potential to indirectly improve mental stability and clarity by reducing systemic inflammation.

Important Stressors Associated with Depression and Anxiety Relief

Certain probiotic strains have demonstrated potential in reducing the symptoms of anxiety and depression, but not all probiotics have the same impact on mental health. The most researched strains include:

- It has been demonstrated that Lactobacillus rhamnosus possesses anxiolytic (anxiety-reducing) properties, most likely through affecting serotonin and GABA synthesis. Researchers are investigating Lactobacillus rhamnosus's potential for treating mood problems in people after finding that it can change behavior in animals by modifying the gut-brain axis.

- **Bifidobacterium longum:** Research has indicated that by regulating inflammatory pathways and immunological responses, Bifidobacterium longum may help lower stress and anxiety. It is believed to increase the synthesis of neurotransmitters such as GABA and serotonin, which affects mood management and mental clarity.

- **Lactobacillus helveticus:** Research has been done on this strain's potential antidepressant benefits. Supplementing with Lactobacillus helveticus has been associated in clinical trials with mood enhancements, decreased anxiety, and improved sleep quality.

- **Bifidobacterium bifidum:** Known for balancing gut flora, Bifidobacterium bifidum has been linked to reduced symptoms of depression and enhanced cognitive performance.

Early human trials and animal models have demonstrated the potential of these strains, and ongoing research is confirming their effectiveness in treating mental health conditions.

7.2 Food Sources versus Supplements

When it comes to adding psychobiotics to their diet, people frequently have to choose between using probiotic-rich foods or probiotic pills. Although each strategy offers unique advantages and possible disadvantages, both choices have advantages.

The Benefits and Drawbacks of Supplement Use

Probiotic supplements can provide targeted dosages of particular bacterial strains and are generally accessible. Usually sold as supplements to enhance mental and digestive health, these products come in liquid, powder, or capsule form. The following are the main benefits and drawbacks of probiotic supplementation:

Advantages:

- **Simplicity:** Supplements offer a steady and regulated dosage of good bacteria and are simple to include into everyday schedules.
- **Targeted Strains:** A lot of supplements include

particular probiotic strains that have been demonstrated to improve mental health, enabling people to meet their personal needs.

- **larger Potency:** Probiotics are frequently found in larger concentrations in supplements than in food, which may result in more rapid or powerful effects.

Cons:

- **Lack of Regulation:** Probiotic supplement quality, potency, and purity can vary greatly because the supplement market is not as strictly controlled as the pharmaceutical sector.
- **Possible Side Effects:** When starting probiotics, some people may have moderate stomach discomfort, gas, or bloating.
- **Cost:** Probiotic supplements, especially premium or specialist strains, can be pricey.

Natural Psychobiotics from Fermented Foods

Since ancient times, people have used fermented foods for their health advantages and as a natural supply of probiotics. A healthy gut microbiota can be supported by the abundance of living bacteria found in certain meals.

Compared to supplements, fermented foods may have the following benefits:

Pros:

- **Natural Source:** A range of probiotic strains found in fermented foods, including kimchi, sauerkraut, kefir, kombucha, and yogurt, can improve both brain and digestive health.

- **Packed with Nutrients:** Fermented foods are frequently high in vitamins, minerals, and antioxidants that promote general health and wellbeing, in addition to probiotics.

- **Dietary Synergy**: Including fermented foods in a balanced diet adds extra nutrients that may enhance the effects of probiotics by complementing their advantages.

Cons:

- **Variable Strain Composition:** The strain composition of fermented foods might change based on the fermentation process, in contrast to pills that provide a fixed dosage of probiotics. Controlling the consumption of particular probiotic strains associated with mental health benefits becomes more challenging as a result.

- **Potential Allergens**: People who are lactose intolerant or allergic to milk may not be able to consume certain fermented foods, such as dairy-based goods.

- **Process of Fermentation:** Not every fermented food is made equally. The beneficial bacteria may be killed during the pasteurization process of some commercially produced varieties, reducing their effectiveness.

A more comprehensive approach to gut health is offered by fermented foods, which contain a variety of probiotics and other advantageous substances including prebiotics that support the development of good bacteria.

7.3 Psychobiotics' Clinical Support

Numerous clinical investigations that seek to understand how probiotics can affect mental health have been sparked by the growing interest in psychobiotics. Studies have mostly examined the effects of particular strains, such

Lactobacillus and Bifidobacterium, on anxiety, depression, and mood regulation in general.

Research on Bifidobacterium and Lactobacillus Strains

The effectiveness of psychobiotics in enhancing mental health outcomes has been demonstrated by numerous studies. Animals and humans who took Lactobacillus rhamnosus supplements showed less anxiety-like behavior, according to a 2016 study published in Psychiatry Research. The study showed that the probiotics changed the expression of genes linked to anxiety and directly affected the gut-brain axis.

It has also been demonstrated that Bifidobacterium longum improves stress and depression. Bifidobacterium supplementation was shown to alleviate depressive symptoms in people with major depressive disorder in a randomized controlled experiment that was reported in JAMA Psychiatry.

Extended Effects on Mental Health Results

Although research on the long-term impact of psychobiotics on mental health is ongoing, preliminary findings indicate that regular use may provide long-lasting advantages. Participants in a long-term trial on the use of Lactobacillus helveticus for depression reported an overall increase in quality of life in addition to a decrease in depressive symptoms after taking the probiotic for several months.

These preliminary results imply that probiotics may be a useful adjunct therapy for those looking to manage chronic mental health issues like anxiety and depression, even if additional study is required to prove the long-term effects of psychobiotics.

A natural and perhaps successful method of treating anxiety, depression, and other mood disorders, psychobiotics represent a promising new area in mental health care. Certain probiotic strains have been demonstrated to affect neurotransmitter synthesis, lower inflammation, and control stress responses via modifying the gut-brain axis. Psychobiotics can provide beneficial support for mental health, whether taken as supplements or via fermented foods. Together with conventional therapy, psychobiotics may play a significant role in comprehensive mental health care methods as clinical data grows.

CHAPTER 8

LEAKY GUT SYNDROME RECOVERY

The condition known as Leaky Gut Syndrome has drawn more attention recently because of its possible connection to a number of illnesses, including mental health conditions and digestive problems. Fundamentally, Leaky Gut describes the gut lining's weakened state, which permits toxic chemicals to enter the bloodstream and sets off an inflammatory reaction. This chapter offers a thorough explanation of Leaky Gut Syndrome, including its causes, consequences on brain function, and the procedures needed to repair the gut lining and regain health. Along with discussing practical methods for repairing the gut and reducing systemic inflammation, we will also look at the relationship between Leaky Gut, autoimmune diseases, and mood disorders.

8.1 Leaky Gut Syndrome: What Is It?

A disorder known as "Leaky Gut Syndrome" causes damage to the small intestine's lining, which raises intestinal permeability. Because of this malfunction, poisons, dangerous microorganisms, and undigested food particles can "leak" through the intestinal lining and into the circulation. The gut lining normally functions as a selective barrier, letting vital nutrients into the bloodstream while blocking toxic chemicals. However, this barrier is weakened in people with Leaky Gut, which results in a number of systemic problems.

Factors Contributing to Systemic Inflammation

Leaky Gut Syndrome has multiple etiological components, including genetic and environmental influences. Among the key contributors are:

- The balance of gut microbiota can be upset by diets high in processed foods, sweets, and unhealthy fats, which can lead to inflammation and a compromised intestinal barrier. Gut permeability can be exacerbated by consuming a lot of inflammatory foods, such as refined carbs, artificial additives, and excessive alcohol.

- By changing the gut flora and raising gut permeability, psychological and physical stress can have a detrimental impact on gut health. The inflammatory reaction that stress triggers in the body can harm intestinal cell tight junctions and encourage leaky gut.

- **Infections:** Inflammation of the gut, resulting in an imbalance of gut bacteria and compromising intestinal lining integrity, can be caused by bacterial, viral, and parasite infections. Particularly, pathogens like Candida albicans and Helicobacter pylori have been connected to increased intestinal permeability.

- **Medications:** Antibiotics, nonsteroidal anti-inflammatory medicines (NSAIDs), and other pharmacological medications can cause disruptions to the intestinal lining. For example, chronic NSAID use can harm the intestinal mucosa, resulting in inflammation and increased intestinal permeability.

These elements combine to damage the intestinal barrier,

which causes systemic inflammation. The development of numerous illnesses, including autoimmune diseases, gastrointestinal disorders, and even neurological and mood-related problems, is subsequently facilitated by this inflammation.

How It Impacts Brain Activity

The gut-brain axis the possible impact of Leaky Gut on brain function, is one of the most worrisome side effects. Signals can go between the gut and the brain thanks to this communication channel. Dangerous substances can enter the bloodstream and cause an immunological reaction when the stomach lining becomes porous. The production of inflammatory chemicals called cytokines as a result of this immune activity can reach the brain and disrupt its normal function.

- Leaky Gut inflammation has been linked to the development of neuroinflammation, a disorder in which the brain becomes inflamed, according to studies. Numerous neurological and mental conditions have been connected to neuroinflammation, including:

- **sadness:** Mood disorders like sadness and anxiety can be exacerbated by inflammation in the brain, which can change the balance of neurotransmitters like serotonin and dopamine.

- **Cognitive Decline:** Prolonged inflammation in the brain can affect cognitive function, resulting in attention issues, memory issues, and brain fog.

- Leaky Gut may contribute to the onset or aggravation of autism spectrum disorders (ASD) by altering brain function via inflammatory pathways, according to new research.

- It is feasible to lower inflammation and enhance gut and brain health by repairing the integrity of the gut lining, which will enhance general wellbeing.

8.2 Gut Lining Repair Procedures

A diversified strategy is needed to treat Leaky Gut Syndrome, with an emphasis on both intestinal lining repair and the root causes of gut permeability. The methods listed below have been shown to be successful in lowering inflammation and reestablishing gut health.

Nutritional Strategies (e.g., Collagen, L-Glutamine)

In order to promote the healing of the intestinal lining, nutrition is essential. It has been determined that the following nutrients and supplements help to build the intestinal barrier and aid in healing:

- **L-Glutamine:** An amino acid called L-glutamine is the main source of energy for intestinal cells. It supports the function of the gut epithelial cells, which helps preserve the integrity of the intestinal lining. L-glutamine supplements have been demonstrated to improve gut function and decrease intestinal permeability, particularly in people with Leaky Gut.

- **Collagen:** Collagen is a vital protein that maintains the gut lining's structure. Glycine and proline, two amino acids found in it, aid in tissue repair and inflammation reduction. Supplementing with collagen has been shown to help repair gut integrity and encourage intestinal lining recovery.

- **Zinc:** Zinc is essential for intestinal barrier repair and immunological function. Increased intestinal permeability has been associated with zinc deficiency; supplementation may help lower inflammation and leaking in the gut.

- Fish oils and plant-based sources such as flaxseeds include omega-3 fatty acids, which have anti-inflammatory qualities. They support the healing process for people with Leaky Gut by lowering systemic inflammation and regulating the immune system.

- The gut can be shielded from inflammation and oxidative stress by flavonoids and other antioxidants, such as vitamins A, C, and E. These nutrients support gut lining healing and aid in the repair of damaged cells.

- Repairing the gut lining and lowering gut

permeability can be greatly aided by including these nutrients in the diet through food and supplements.

Steer clear of triggers like alcohol and NSAIDs

Healing requires not only nutritional support but also avoiding chemicals that can exacerbate damage to the gut lining. Important triggers to stay away from are:

- **NSAIDs:** Ibuprofen and aspirin are two examples of nonsteroidal anti-inflammatory medicines (NSAIDs), which are frequently used to treat pain and inflammation. On the other hand, long-term NSAID use can harm the intestinal mucosa and encourage leaky gut. In order to promote gut healing, NSAID use must be reduced or stopped.

- **Alcohol:** Long-term alcohol use has been linked to increased permeability, impaired motility, and damage to the gut lining. Alcohol is a crucial trigger to avoid when repairing Leaky Gut since it not only upsets the delicate balance of gut bacteria but also makes inflammation worse.

- **Processed Foods**: Foods that have been processed and contain harmful fats, refined sugars, and artificial additives can aggravate intestinal permeability and cause inflammation. For gut healing, a whole-foods-based, anti-inflammatory diet is crucial.

The intestinal lining can progressively mend by removing these triggers and providing the gut with nutrients that promote healing, which will enhance both mental and digestive health.

8.3 The Relationship Between Mood and Autoimmune Disorders

Because of the intimate connection between the immune system and the gut, Leaky Gut Syndrome is intimately linked to mood disorders and autoimmune diseases. Undigested food particles, poisons, and viruses can enter the bloodstream through damaged gut lining, which can set off an immunological reaction. This persistent immunological stimulation has the potential to cause autoimmune diseases and mental disorders over time.

Communication Between the Brain and Immune System

Much of the body's immune system is located in the gut, and immune function is closely related to gut health. Damage to the gut lining triggers the immune system, which results in the creation of inflammatory cytokines and autoantibodies. These chemicals may contribute to neuroinflammation in the brain after traveling throughout the body.

Numerous mood and cognitive disorders, such as depression, anxiety, and autoimmune encephalitis, have been associated with neuroinflammation. The gut's continuous signals of inflammation can change the chemistry of the brain, causing problems with the synthesis of neurotransmitters and affecting mental health.

Resolving Autoimmune Disorders to Maintain Mood

Numerous autoimmune diseases, such as rheumatoid arthritis, lupus, and Hashimoto's thyroiditis, have been linked to Leaky Gut Syndrome. Autoimmune reactions result from the immune system attacking its own tissues when the intestinal barrier is breached. Therefore, by lowering inflammation in the gut and restoring immunological function, Leaky Gut can be a major factor in the management of autoimmune diseases.

Managing autoimmune flare-ups and enhancing general mental health can be achieved by repairing the gut lining, lowering inflammation, and reestablishing immunological equilibrium. Furthermore, addressing underlying gut dysfunction might lessen the brain's inflammatory load, promoting mood stability and easing anxiety and depressive symptoms.

Leaky Gut Syndrome is a multifaceted illness that has significant effects on one's physical and mental well-being. People can take preventative measures to heal the gut lining and lessen systemic inflammation by being aware of its sources and the ways it impacts the body. A thorough healing strategy must include nutritional strategies, trigger avoidance, and attention to the gut-brain link. Restoring gut health is still essential to attaining overall wellness as studies into the connection between Leaky Gut and autoimmune/mood disorders continue. The gut can be repaired, the immune system can be balanced, and eventually mental and physical health can be enhanced by certain protocols and lifestyle modifications.

CHAPTER 9

Gut-Brain Connection Personalized Medicine

Both mental and physical health are significantly impacted by the complex and dynamic gut-brain link. A one-size-fits-all approach to healthcare is insufficient for addressing complex ailments including mental health disorders, autoimmune diseases, and chronic illnesses, as research continues to advance. Targeting each patient's specific needs based on genetic, microbiological, and lifestyle characteristics, personalized medicine offers a novel and customized approach to treatment, especially when it comes to gut health. With an emphasis on integrating mental health techniques, customizing interventions, and monitoring progress for long-term success, this chapter explores the significance of personalized medicine in comprehending and enhancing the gut-brain relationship.

9.1 Adapting Interventions to Specific Requirements

The goal behind personalized medicine is to tailor treatment plans according to each person's particular genetic composition, microbiome composition, and environmental circumstances. Personalized interventions provide a more focused and efficient approach than generic treatments when it comes to gut health and its effects on the brain. Healthcare professionals can create a customized treatment plan that targets the underlying causes of gut dysfunction and its impact on mental health by recognizing particular needs and imbalances.

Genetic Testing's Function in Treating Microbiomes

Understanding a person's gut health and how it relates to mental health is mostly dependent on genetic testing. Genetic variables that affect how the body handles nutrients, tolerates food, and reacts to external stressors also affect the human microbiome, which is the diverse population of microbes that live in the gut. Healthcare professionals can find genetic predispositions that may affect the balance of gut microbiota and how it interacts with the brain by examining a person's genome.

For instance, both mental and digestive health may be impacted by genetic variations in genes that produce neurotransmitters like dopamine, serotonin, and GABA (gamma-aminobutyric acid). These differences can be identified by personalized genetic testing, which aids in customizing treatments aimed at reestablishing the balance of the microbiome and reducing related emotional or cognitive disorders. A customized approach is especially important for successful treatment because certain people may have genetic predispositions that make them more vulnerable to diseases like anxiety, depression, or irritable bowel syndrome (IBS).

Furthermore, polymorphisms in immune system-related genes that may contribute to disorders like neuroinflammation or autoimmune diseases can be found with the aid of genetic testing. People who have a certain IL-6 gene mutation, for example, may have an inflated immune response, which can lead to persistent inflammation in the brain and stomach. More accurate treatment of inflammatory diseases that impact the gut-brain axis is made possible by an understanding of these hereditary predispositions.

Customized Prebiotics and Probiotics

Although it is commonly known that probiotics and prebiotics can improve gut health, not all strains and varieties are good for everyone. Taking into consideration a person's particular gut bacterial composition and genetic predispositions, personalized probiotics and prebiotics are made to support their own microbiome.

When taken in sufficient quantities, probiotics live microorganisms produce health advantages, usually through enhancing or reestablishing the gut flora. It has been demonstrated that some probiotic strains, such Lactobacillus and Bifidobacterium, promote gut health and have an impact on mental health, especially by modifying the gut-brain axis. But not everyone responds well to every strain, and some people may even experience discomfort or worsen their problems. Based on a person's unique gut bacterial makeup, personalized microbiome testing can identify the probiotic strains that are most likely to be helpful.

Conversely, prebiotics are indigestible fibers that support the development and function of good gut flora. Healthcare professionals may make sure that people are getting the proper kinds and quantities of fibers that will specifically promote the growth of beneficial gut flora by customizing prebiotic supplements. For example, a prebiotic supplement that promotes the growth of particular microorganisms without producing symptoms may be helpful for those with inflammatory bowel disease (IBD) or IBS.

The gut microbiome is balanced and optimized for both digestive and mental health when probiotics and prebiotics are customized to meet each person's specific needs. In addition to enhancing gut health, this individualized strategy may improve the course of diseases including anxiety, depression, and cognitive loss.

9.2 Mental Health Integrative Approaches

Personalized medicine takes mental health into consideration in addition to physical health. Traditional psychiatric treatments are combined with complementary therapies that address underlying lifestyle, nutritional, and gut health issues in integrative approaches to mental health. People can recover more comprehensively and sustainably by combining techniques that promote mental health and heal the stomach.

Integrating Gut-Healing Techniques with Psychotherapy

A proven treatment for a variety of mental health issues, such as anxiety, depression, and trauma, is psychotherapy. However, the efficacy of psychotherapy can be increased when paired with techniques meant to repair the gut and restore the microbiome. Instead of merely treating the symptoms of mental health disorders, this approach tackles their underlying causes.

For instance, by assisting patients in identifying and altering harmful thought patterns, cognitive-behavioral therapy (CBT) is frequently used to treat anxiety and depression. Nonetheless, optimizing the brain's neurochemical balance through gut-healing measures like probiotic supplements, dietary modifications, and stress-relieving exercises (like yoga or mindfulness) can enhance the advantages of psychotherapy.

Additionally, the gut-brain axis is a two-way street: an imbalanced gut microbiome can exacerbate mental health, while psychological stress can cause alterations in the gut microbiome. Integrative techniques provide a more thorough and efficient treatment plan by treating both the psychological and physiological aspects of mental health.

Multidisciplinary Care's Advantages

The participation of several medical specialists, each of whom offers their specialization to the healing process, is one of the main benefits of integrative treatments. Providing multidisciplinary care requires cooperation between:

- Psychiatrists and therapists who specialize in treating mental health issues; Nutritionists and dietitians who offer dietary recommendations specific to gut health; Gastroenterologists who identify and treat disorders relating to the gut; and Integrative medicine practitioners who might provide complementary therapies like acupuncture, herbal medicine, or mindfulness exercises.

- This all-encompassing strategy guarantees that every facet of an individual's health from the intellect to the microbiome is taken care of. For instance, a gastroenterologist may treat any underlying digestive diseases, a nutritionist may offer guidance on foods that promote gut healing, and a therapist may help a patient manage stress. Better long-term results and increased general well-being can arise from the combination of these strategies.

9.3 Monitoring and Modifying for Extended Achievement

In order to achieve long-term success, personalized medicine is a continual process that necessitates constant monitoring and modification. Through the use of wearable technology, symptom tracking, and frequent check-ins with medical professionals, people may monitor their mental and intestinal health and make necessary modifications.

Employing Wearable Technology and Symptom

Trackers

A key component of personalized treatment is symptom tracking, which enables the patient and the healthcare professional to track development and spot any setbacks or advancements. People can record their experiences with mental health (such as anxiety, sadness, and brain fog) and digestive health (such as bloating, constipation, and diarrhea) using symptom trackers. These monitors can offer important information about how lifestyle adjustments, food adjustments, and supplementation affect symptoms.

Wearable technology, such as fitness trackers or biofeedback devices, can assist people in tracking physical health indicators that are related to gut-brain health in addition to symptom trackers. For example, wearable technology may monitor physical activity, heart rate variability, stress levels, and sleep patterns all of which have an impact on mental and intestinal health. With the use of these gadgets, people can gather data in real time and modify their treatments or routines in response to feedback.

Frequent Consultations with Medical Experts

For tailored treatment to succeed in the long run, regular discussions with medical experts are crucial. These check-ins make it possible to continuously assess patient progress, adjust treatment plans, and, if necessary, identify new interventions. In order to modify treatment regimens as needed, medical professionals can examine data from wearable devices, test results, and symptom monitors.

Professionals can also provide invaluable assistance in overcoming obstacles, such as when new symptoms appear or the body may not react as anticipated to specific treatments. Frequent check-ups guarantee that people are maintaining their course and consistently improving their gut-brain health for long-term wellbeing.

A fundamental shift in the way we treat gut and mental health is represented by personalized medicine. We can develop more efficient, focused therapy programs that target the underlying causes of mental health issues and gut dysfunction by customizing therapies based on each patient's unique genetic, microbial, and environmental characteristics. Integrative methods, which combine gut-healing techniques with psychotherapy, provide a comprehensive road to recovery, and monitoring and modifying for long-term success guarantees long-lasting progress. This individualized approach, which prioritizes each person's particular needs and leads to better outcomes and a more thorough understanding of the gut-brain link, is the way of the future for healthcare.

CHAPTER 10

GUT-BRAIN RESEARCH AND APPLICATIONS IN THE FUTURE

In recent years, the gut-brain axis, the link between the gut and the brain, has attracted a lot of interest, offering important new insights into the interactions and influences between the two systems. The future of gut-brain health seems bright as long as research keeps moving forward, especially when new scientific discoveries, therapies, and technology open the door to creative cures and preventative strategies. The future of gut-brain research is examined in this chapter, with particular attention paid to developments in microbiome analysis, new treatments, and useful lessons that people may apply to their everyday lives to maximize gut health for mental health.

10.1 Developments in the Analysis of Microbiomes

The study of the gut-brain axis now revolves around an understanding of the microbiome, which is the collection of trillions of microorganisms that live in our gut. The sophisticated instruments and technology that enable a more thorough, in-depth examination of the microbiome hold the key to the future of gut-brain research. These developments will not only improve our knowledge of how the gut affects mental health, but they will also make it possible to treat patients more precisely and individually.

Artificial Intelligence in Diagnostics for Gut Health

Microbiome analysis is only one of the many areas of healthcare that artificial intelligence (AI) is transforming. Large volumes of microbiome data are being analyzed more quickly and precisely using AI-driven technologies, like machine learning algorithms, than with conventional techniques. AI can recognize intricate patterns in gut bacteria that are connected to a number of illnesses, such as autoimmune diseases, mood disorders, and gastrointestinal problems, by analyzing data from DNA sequencing.

AI can, for instance, search through massive datasets to find microbial signatures linked to mental health issues like anxiety and depression. This allows for a more individualized diagnosis approach by predicting which bacterial profiles may be connected to a person's symptoms. AI may also assist in monitoring changes over time by offering continuous evaluations of a person's gut microbiota to see how it reacts to treatments like probiotics, diet, or medicine. Treatments for gut health could be revolutionized by this individualized diagnostic technique, which offers tailored therapy based on each individual's unique microbiome composition.

Additionally, by examining a person's genetic information, lifestyle choices, and microbiological profiles, AI can assist in forecasting how they will react to specific treatments. This can greatly improve outcomes for gut function and mental health by enabling more rapid and precise interventions that are customized to the individual's particular needs.

The Significance of Metagenomics

Researchers can examine the whole microbial community in the gut by using metagenomics, the study of genetic material extracted directly from environmental samples like stool. In contrast to conventional microbiome research, which concentrates on cultivating certain bacteria, metagenomics can offer a thorough picture of all microbial species found in the gastrointestinal system, including bacteria, viruses, fungus, and archaea.

This method provides insights into how the diversity and abundance of particular bacteria impact the gut's capacity to interact with the brain, which has significant ramifications for comprehending the gut-brain axis. For instance, metagenomics research has previously shown that some gut bacteria, such as those belonging to the Firmicutes and Bacteroidetes phyla, are linked to a number of mental health conditions, such as autism spectrum disorders, anxiety, and depression. Researchers can find new therapy targets, such probiotics, prebiotics, or other microbiome-modulating medicines that can affect mental health, by identifying these microbial profiles.

Future developments in metagenomics and sophisticated computational techniques may make it easier to develop customized microbiome treatments, providing a more sophisticated and customized method of regulating gut-brain health. Treatments for autoimmune diseases, metabolic disorders, and even neurodegenerative diseases like Alzheimer's disease may be impacted by this, which could go beyond mental health.

10.2 Emerging Treatment Systems

Researchers are creating new treatments that take advantage of our growing understanding of the gut microbiome's significant influence on mental health in order to enhance mental health. Although many of these treatments are still in the early phases of clinical testing, they present encouraging prospects for treatments in the future that go beyond conventional pharmacological methods.

Transplanting Fecal Microbiota (FMT) for Mental Health

The purpose of fecal microbiota transplantation (FMT) is to restore a balanced microbiome by introducing a sample of a donor's healthy gut microbiota into the patient's digestive tract. FMT was first used to treat Clostridium difficile infections, but it has since drawn interest as a possible treatment for a variety of illnesses, including mental health issues.

The idea behind FMT's application to mental health is that disorders like anxiety, depression, and even neurodegenerative illnesses may be exacerbated by gut dysbiosis, or an imbalance in the gut flora. FMT has demonstrated promise in treating mood disorders, lowering stress levels, and possibly boosting cognitive function by reestablishing a diverse and healthy microbiota. Although more thorough research is required to validate its efficacy and safety, preliminary studies have indicated that the transfer of microbiota from healthy donors can significantly influence mood and behavior in individuals with diseases like depression.

As more study is done on FMT for mental health, it might be accepted as a therapeutic option and provide a viable substitute for conventional psychiatric drugs, which frequently have negative side effects. More research is needed to ascertain the long-term effects, ideal donor selection standards, and best techniques for treatment administration before FMT can be widely adopted.

Clinical Trials of Gut-Brain Modulators

Developing gut-brain modulators is another exciting field of study. These are medicinal substances made to target particular gut-brain axis pathways in order to alter the two systems' communication and enhance mental health results. Gut-brain modulators seek to restore equilibrium in the microbiota and its impact on the brain, in contrast to conventional psychiatric drugs that frequently concentrate on changing brain chemistry.

The use of probiotics, prebiotics, and postbiotics (compounds created by probiotics) are among the clinical investigations that are now examining the potential of these modulators. By enhancing gut health and lowering systemic inflammation, certain probiotic strains have been found in some trials to help reduce the symptoms of anxiety and depression. In the future, gut-brain modulators that target the underlying gut imbalances that cause mood disorders may offer a more direct and efficient way to treat mental health conditions.

In order to provide a comprehensive approach to mental health that takes into account both the stomach and the brain, these therapies could also be utilized in conjunction with conventional treatments like psychotherapy and lifestyle modifications.

10.3 Useful Lessons for Daily Living

There are doable actions people can take today to enhance their gut health and, in turn, their mental health, even as ground-breaking research and novel treatments are in the works. Giving people information on the gut-brain link empowers them to make decisions that could improve their health and well-being in the long run.

Encouraging People to Make Gut-Friendly Decisions
Making gut-friendly decisions entails embracing a food and way of life that promotes a balanced microbiota. The following useful advice can help to boost mental health and intestinal health:

- Eating a varied, high-fiber diet: The fiber and nutrients needed to support good gut bacteria are found in a diet high in fruits, vegetables, whole grains, and legumes. Plant-based food diversity promotes a diverse microbiome, which is essential for mental well-being.

- Take Fermented Foods into Account: Probiotics, found in foods like yogurt, kefir, kimchi, sauerkraut, and kombucha, help the gut's good bacteria proliferate. Eating fermented foods on a regular basis can help with mood disorders and intestinal health.

- Reduce Sugar and Processed Foods: Diets high in processed foods, sweets, and chemical additives can exacerbate inflammation and gut dysbiosis, both of which have a detrimental effect on mental health. A balanced microbiota is maintained by consuming less of these items.

- Engage in stress-relieving activities: Prolonged stress can exacerbate mental health issues and alter the gut microbiota. Regular exercise, yoga, meditation, and mindfulness techniques can all help lower stress and support a positive gut-brain connection.

The Contagious Impact of Better Digestive Health on Mental Health

Beyond merely enhancing digestive health, improving gut

health through dietary adjustments, lifestyle changes, and new treatments can have profound advantages. People may see gains in their mood, cognitive abilities, and general mental health by maintaining a balanced microbiome. A healthy gut microbiota can improve brain function and emotional modulation by lowering inflammation, regulating the generation of neurotransmitters, and maintaining the integrity of the blood-brain barrier.

People will be encouraged to emphasize gut health as a crucial aspect of general well-being as scientific research on the gut-brain relationship in mental health continues to advance.

Research on the gut-brain relationship has enormous promise for advancing our knowledge of how the microbiota affects mental health and for using this insight to create novel treatments. Metagenomics and AI-driven diagnostics are two developments in microbiome analysis that are opening the door to more individualized and accurate treatments. In the meanwhile, there is hope for more successful treatments for mental health conditions thanks to novel medicines like FMT and gut-brain modulators. People can take practical measures to enhance their gut health in the interim by making dietary, stress-reduction, and lifestyle changes. In the end, they will benefit from a healthier gut and a more balanced mind. The gut-brain link will surely become a fundamental aspect of mental health study and therapy in the years to come as science advances.

ABOUT THE AUTHOR

 Harmony Royce is a dedicated healthcare worker who has a strong interest in holistic wellness. Harmony's extensive history in various aspects of health and wellness provides her with a wealth of knowledge and expertise that she can utilize in her writing and professional endeavors.

Harmony is a talented author who crafts thought-provoking books that inspire readers to have well-rounded, balanced lives. She writes about a variety of health-related topics, such as diet, exercise, mental health, and mindfulness. Her approachable writing style combines practical guidance with evidence-based research to make complex health concepts approachable and engaging for readers of all ages.

Harmony actively promotes the benefits of holistic health through writing, community workshops, and internet forums. Her mission is to educate and inspire people about the transformative power of self-care and healthy lifestyle choices.

www.ingramcontent.com/pod-product-compliance
Lightning Source LLC
Chambersburg PA
CBHW071039250726
48653CB00005B/1904